The Things I Think I Think: Part One

(Hopeful Wisdom and Advice for You to Apply)

By Ben Donley

DreamLoud Publishing

Copyright © 2020

Published 2021

All rights reserved. No part of this book may be reproduced, stored in a retrieval system, or transmitted in any form or by any means, electronic, mechanical, photocopying, recording, or otherwise without the written permission of DreamLoud Publishing.

Printed in the United States of America

The Things I Think I Think | Ben Donley

Dedicated to Blaise Pascal

Your *Pensées* inspired this *Bensées*

Self-Disclosure and Disclaimer

This is a book of proverbs, aphorisms, advice, truth, humor and attempted wisdom. But it was written by me — a wretched sinner who has foolishly failed in more ways than most.

I just want to be clear from the outset that I <u>do</u> know I am an idiot.

I have not written this book to promote myself as a holy sage who has lived out my own wisdom well.

The main reason I share the following is to challenge you to both know well and then, unlike me, to do well. You see, I always knew better, but I didn't do better. And that is an important truth to swallow. You can be given wisdom by **God**, share that wisdom, but not live by that wisdom.

You can know what's best and then always do what is worst.

Any doubts? Ask King Solomon — he was the wisest man ever and yet he used his free will to make the most horrific decisions available. (But he did write out some really powerful proverbs we can all use.)

And while I have also made my mistakes, I too believe I have some useful offerings for you. I wrote this book to tell you what I think is important to do and think and say and pray during the life you have.

Know better, do better and live your best.

So, enjoy my fairly random advice and see what it looks like upon application. Take what you think is useful and put it into practice. Then, write your own book about

The Things I Think I Think | Ben Donley

the things you think you think and pass it on to the ones you love.

Think you can do that?

Might be fun, right?

The Things I Think I Think

Part One: Aphorisms, Proverbs, Advice

Per'speck'tive

Before we get to my thoughts, let's consider how I view the world. I call this my per'speck'tive.

My per'speck'tive gives me a basic framework so I am able to respond to people and circumstances in consistent ways so I can be happy at the end of each day.

I force my thoughts, feelings, actions, every circumstance and every person to pass through these filters. I have found this action helpful in reducing my daily stress, pressure and fear.

My Per'speck'tive

-I am just a speck. One of seven billion on a tiny planet in a tiny galaxy within a huge universe who is following the lead of generations of billions who have set up a game board for us, but who are now dead.

-As a speck, I do mostly smaller speck-level things. Speck-level things are mostly minuscule. There are no **BIG** things, even if other specks tell me there are. So, while I must do speck-level things every day of my life, I won't super-size any of them despite others' claims there is a lot riding on a specific speck-task. This removes any personal pressure or stress. I can act freely, do my best to create positive outcomes and never worry about how those outcomes actually land.

(There is no big game, big meeting, big test, big _____. How we elevate the consequences tied to the event or task will determine if we see anything as big or small. Fear of "our" worst-case scenarios, which is usually tied to insecurities which are often tied to real traumas, drives this elevation! "Who cares?" and "So what?" are key phrases to use a lot in our thoughts that drive our emotions and actions.)

-My proper speck-level sizing is based on this: Everything I do that is not for God's glory or under His command is meaningless. While it may have an effect, it holds no real importance. Most of life is a silly game. Speck-stuff is just chasing after the wind.

-Many specks around me don't think like I do, and thus, they try to be the biggest speck-fish in the biggest speck-ponds, chasing after game objectives I could not care less about. They might even try all sorts of manipulative tactics and form various sketchy alliances to gain control of larger sections of this planetary game board. I won't judge them, but I won't be fooled into elevating the small things or small people to places of significance like they do.

-Speck-media, speck-politicians and speck-marketers exist to super-spin and super-size issues and products so I will care about them enough to give them my attention and my money. I appreciate them trying to distract me from the boredom of this life, but I will mostly ignore their pleas.

-Speck-products can be entertaining, useful, convenient and/or exciting. But they are really not worth much in the long run. So, I will own some speck-products but will always be willing to leave them behind at the drop of a hat. I'll not hold too tightly to that which I cannot take with me beyond this planet.

-Knowing that other people outside of media and marketing are also specks, I don't have to care too much what they think about me. People's perceptions are flawed because their experience and knowledge are limited. I will not give myself over to them whether they think me worthy of kingship or martyrdom. My identity as God's loved speck is set and no other speck can add to that or subtract from it.

-All specks are created by and loved by God and thus must be loved by me. Seeing myself as but a speck makes it easier to be humble and even to lay down my speck-life for those around me.

-My speck-death is imminent. During the time I do have, I want to be a humble and grateful speck who uses what God has given me to impact the lives of the neediest specks within my sphere of influence, especially with regards to their eternal future.

-As a speck, I will not be remembered for very long after my death. Making speck-history is not my goal. I'm not here to have buildings named after me. I don't even want or need a quality obituary or eulogy. As long as the speck-Maker remembers me on the other side, I am good to go. This saves me from trying to do what is "memorable" and frees me up to do what is kind and just.

(Most specks, even the most ripple-causing, intelligent and famous specks, are forgotten long before their deaths. Specks tend to 'radar-blip,' then fade.)

-I have a lot in common with the specks around me (loss, pain, troubles, options, preferences, families, traumas, stresses, barriers, temptations, desires, etc.), but what they are after, I am not. Still, it is good to think of my other specks as more similar to me than completely different from me. Our shared realities help form the basis of my re'speck't for others.

-Most specks I know chase after the following "game" objectives: Pleasure, Power, Influence, Fame, Wealth, Love, Happiness, Health, Purpose/Meaning, Strength, Beauty, Style, Spirituality, Intelligence and/or Possessions, and I will be tempted to go after them, too. But since the methods used to achieve them are typically joyless and busy grabs for what falls short of any version of lasting satisfaction (*The Matrix* Blue Pill), I pray I quickly notice any shifts of MO and exit ramp back onto my narrow, alien path toward deeper satisfaction.

-No other speck can ruin my life. They might ruin moments or seasons, but I have the choice to respond with resilience and grace.

-Some specks may try to hurt me, control me and/or use me for their base ends, but I choose whether or not to let them.

-My speck-life is guided by the Bible, and thus, I need to know what the point of the Bible is: to introduce me to God, Jesus and the Holy Spirit and to show me how to gain and maintain intimacy with them. As well, it tells me what I can be certain of no matter what is happening in my world. Faith is certainty. I must ask daily, what am I certain of and why am I uncertain of other things? Do I have a 'no matter what' kind of faith or an 'if this, then' type of faith?

(My "certainty" will be tested so I will probably find out.)

The Things I Think I Think

Now, let's proceed to the things I think I think about both the deep and the shallow.

(Take these thoughts as my best advice on how to live a best life.)

The Deeper End

--You get a big say in determining what kind of movie your life will be. You almost always have a choice of how your scenes will look. You are the writer, actor and casting director. Don't be a horror flick.

--You have intrinsic worth. God said He made you in His image and loves you. Stop wasting your time trying to prove yourself to fellow creatures.

--Love yourself. Love others.

--Don't be a performance junkie. Pleasing people is a soul-crusher.

--Just because someone proclaims that something is 'something,' doesn't mean that something is *actually* something.

--Opinions that lead to debate are often based on your limited experiences and float on top of your desperate insecurities. Stop debating. Stop giving your opinions as if they are facts.

--Everyone around you experiences the whole of the human condition: Joy, Depression, Loss, Tragedy, Pain, Brokenness, Discipline, Happiness, Excitement, Enjoyment, Failure, Rejection, Sickness, Unfairness, Power, Change, Inertia, Movement, Oppression, Fear, Victory, Stress...So, have mercy!

--Be as generous as you can every single day. Giving things away in the midst of a selfish and "scarcity" culture is one of the most shocking kindnesses you can show people.

--Watch less TV.

--Do what you have to do to win the heart of your significant other every day, because if you aren't trying, someone else will be attempting to unseat the 'incumbent'.

--God's ways are higher than your ways. So, stop trying to get your way.

--God's thoughts are higher than your thoughts. So, stop trying to figure everything out with your tiny little brain and your minuscule perspective.

--Root out the ways you manipulate others then stop doing those things.

--Never call anything good that God says is evil. And never call anything evil that God says is good. Let the Bible determine what falls into both categories and stop arguing with it.

--Get comfortable saying, "I don't know." Say it more than anything else because you really do not know. "I'm sorry" and "Thank-You" should follow closely behind.

--What the Bible says is dead on. You can put your full faith in what it says about God, life, meaning, salvation, death, resurrection, blessings, etc.

--Don't let the relational wrecks of your past determine the way you act toward others in your present. Get yourself to a spiritual and emotional body shop ASAP.

--Treat old people well and respect them because they have lasted longer than you on this difficult planet.

--Have low expectations for everyone.

--Have low expectations for everything.

--Watch out for those things you judge people for. Often you will do exactly what those people have done and sometimes, even worse.
(Everything I have judged people harshly for, I have now done triple. I'm sure I have out-sinned those I have ripped apart.)

--You can truly taste and see that God is good. When you pray, realize you are entering into God's supernatural sphere and set your expectations accordingly.

--If you're going to call yourself a Christian, don't ever edit, redact, compromise or reduce the Bible into something different so it makes you more comfortable. Believe it and stand on it **ALL** or throw it **ALL** away. Remember, lukewarm gets vomited!

--You will die a horrible death if you eat fast food every day.

--Don't expect much success when trying to fix other people's problems. Most people will say they want help to shift their lives, but they will almost always resent you if you try to help. The majority will not change.

--Find the kindest, most generous, adoring and faithful person possible and make them your best friend. Better yet, become that person for someone else.

--If the words of the Bible make you a jerk to be around, you're not understanding them or applying them correctly.

--Taste buds are not your taste-buddies. They secretly plot against your well-being. Don't give them what they want. Cotton candy and Big Red is a lethal combination. Water is better.

--If Jesus naps during a life storm, you can nap too. Or you can speak to that storm and say with faith, "Peace, be still" and watch the wind and waves die down.

--If you have a mission from God, do it without hesitation, negotiation, complaint, interruption and/or demands.

--Before you get married to anyone, make sure to ask all of the difficult questions and convey all your unpleasant truths.

--Premarital wisdom: Engage in as many different 'stressful' scenarios as you can with your significant other before saying "I Do." If you have only gotten to know them on fun dates and in optimal romantic situations, you probably don't really know them and you are in for some less-than-optimal surprises after the wedding. Know as much as you can before signing on for forever.

--God does not owe you anything.

--What if our nutrient-poor, supermarket food products listed the most likely diseases we would get it if we keep jamming in Yellow #5, Blue #2, MSG, High Fructose Corn Syrup and Aspartame? "Honey, do we want the kids to have only cancer or keep up with the Joneses and Hamburger Helper them all the way to cancer, diabetes *and* IBS?" My gut tells me my 'Honest Box Warnings' would work only as well as Surgeon General's Warnings for cigarettes. I still smoke Pop-Tarts…

--God deals with people as He likes. Put Him in a box and He will blow your box apart. Put Him under a microscope and He will not stay in the shape you expect.

--You can learn from anyone so "people-watch" and "people-listen."

--A person is just a person, regardless of how charismatic, successful, intriguing, popular, degreed or "legitimized" by cultural icons.

--Humans are masters of choice-based self-destruction via self-deception and self-sabotage. We press streaming, subscription darkness into our eyes and thus, our whole beings become filled with darkness. We shovel the most unhealthy foods and drinks into our mouths and thus invest in added weight and potential diseases. Usually, our 'sickness and sin groans' are built on daily drawn freewill blueprints. But truth is, our architecture doesn't have to resemble a tumbledown shanty with burned-out fuses. Choose a different remote control and a better pantry.

--Fast (at least) once a week from your social media and cell phone.

--Go on a spiritual Vision Quest.

--Don't 'need' to be in a relationship with someone so badly that you make self-sabotaging decisions. If someone you love breaks boundaries and is consistently hurting you, walk away.

--You usually earn your reputation, so pay attention to your daily choices.

--Realize that most people don't give a crap about you and rarely think about you. This mindset will free you from worrying about others' perceptions of how you act, look, drive, etc.

--Mostly keep your mouth shut and listen.

--Do justice. Love mercy.

--Don't make decisions based on what you've always done. Things change.

--Life goes on — long after the thrill of living is gone. Just ask Jack or Diane.

--Read great books. Not every book with a reputation for greatness is great.

--If you are a Christian who decides to turn your back on God in favor of a more comfortable cultural belief system, please keep it to yourself. Your insecurity-based attempt to explain your newly deconstructed spiritual placement is a counter to the "good news" of the gospel and is tiresome to those who hear you.

--Write down something you are grateful for every single day.

--Beware of people and governments who ask you to say "yes" to numerous incremental changes that eventually lead to a wholly compromised life.

--Make your 'being' more important than your 'doing'.

--Ask someone more about their lives, give a crap and remember what they talked about for the future — people like to be remembered.

--Don't hold on to trophies or awards from the past, unless they have monetary value. Past wins can crush you in your days of future struggle.

--The masses are easily controlled. Throw fear on them and watch them buckle.

--You live in a corporate oligarchy and have very little power against the money titans, regardless of what democracy asserts. Rage at your own risk.

--Attention, Approval and Applause usually end in character death.

--Don't worry too much about who wins any White House because Presidents have very little power on their own. Until we have our own Nebuchadnezzar or Stalin, don't gripe about how bad a U.S. President is. (God is in control.)

--Zeal without knowledge is a good way to do the 'best' things at the wrong times and in the wrong places. Combine passion and conviction with clear direction from God and you will do what you were meant to do.

--Most people are trying to sell you something.

--Learn how to pray as it says to pray in 2 Corinthians 10:3-5. You are called to demolish enemy strongholds, and in this world, there are plenty of those. Smash every argument that sets itself up against the knowledge of God.

--Beware of strong starts and weak finishes.

--Speak less. Offer fewer opinions. Stop complaining.

--Don't pick on yourself.

--Social Media will make you feel lonelier.

--Think Fast but Decide Slow.

--Political platforms usually only last as long as the general election. Afterward, it's more like "platform diving." And the corporations who funded their winner take over and make their money back. That's history baby.

--God is surely loving and super slow to anger, but just because He is slow to anger doesn't mean you can't drive Him there. Avoid doing that with everything in your power. Beware the deliberate sinning and heed His loving warnings as soon as they come.

--God will usually get your attention using the gentlest techniques possible. His grace and patience are enormous but don't test God.

--Stop trying to be famous.

--Live on as little money as possible.

--Understand that Christianity is not a crutch. It's a leg-breaker and you better count the cost before committing yourself to it.

--Every morning, plan one thing you can look forward to later in the day.

--No matter how mad someone makes you, try to blow it off. Your enemy is not made of flesh and blood.

--Have a strong vocabulary, be a good speller and continuously work on your writing skills.

--The world is not enough. It never will be.

--Clean up your microbiome.

--God owns you. He does not owe you. Stop clamoring for your rights.

--Don't be a slave to your broken self-worth.

--Don't leverage your resources to get ahead in life but leverage your connections to help others climb.

--Don't over-emphasize any verse in the Bible. Allow the entire Bible to speak — not just the things you are comfortable with.

--Be cool with common and simple.

--Fit-out instead of working so hard to fit in.

--Make a real first impression — not a well-plotted, fake one.

--If someone pulls out a gun in a public place where you happen to be, don't duck, cover, and cry. Determine in your heart ahead of time to go down swinging! Be the first to try and overcome them. Be a stopper.

--Live by faith and not by your feelings. How you feel is real, but it's a bad guide. Your feelings are real, but they're not necessarily based on truth. Feelings are nearly always an unreliable guide.

--Become an observer of subcultures and join one...or create one.

--As you probably already know, most formal education is a waste of time as far as the information taught, but school does teach you how to handle deadlines, avoid trouble, manage society, etc.

--Always have hope and persevere. As my close friend says, "Embrace the suck."

--Life will be hard and seem unfair much of the time…but God is an ever-present help when you keep the door open for Him! He'll use those painful experiences to make you into the person He wants you to be.

--Never believe the hype — especially your own.

--If at all possible, eat organic.

--You are probably not as good as you think you are. And you are probably not as bad as you think you are, either.

--Don't spend time thinking about who you used to be. Timeline comparisons are rarely good for your mind.

--Get a truth teller in your life.

--Learn the importance of Ezekiel 9. It absolutely matters that you hate the darkness and evil practices of this fallen world. Get marked by God. Don't conform to the patterns of this planet — stand against them even if people hate you for it.

--Major in college degrees that will get you trained for jobs always needed in society — or skip college, go to a trade school and/or do something thrilling and meaningful.

--You can be super wise but still act super stupid.

--You don't have to repeat the mistakes of your parents. You also don't have to rub their faces in all of their old failures. Cut them some slack and forgive quickly. They were/are just grown-up kids.

--You are a loved child of God.

--Don't assume that the hurts of your life will simply go away with time. Time does not heal all wounds and brokenness doesn't simply reset itself. Pray, journal, get therapy, employ a "life mechanic" — whatever it takes to turn your numerous wounds and wreckages into healed testimonies.

--Don't *need* an apology from anybody for anything. Needing apologies from a human being means you are putting yourself under someone else's control. Don't give anyone that kind of power over you!

--Give people the right to speak into your life — but don't always apply what they say. Test it first.

--Walk away from most controversies and arguments.

--Jesus didn't preach long or 'relevant' sermons. He also didn't preach to get "Amens."

--After reading Revelation, I'm pretty sure that the majority of churches do not qualify as actual churches. Anyone can hang a 'church' sign on a door, but that doesn't make it so.

--No matter what, do not take an Ambien, Lunesta or any hallucinogenic sleeping pill and stay awake. Oh, the horror of the un-remembered post-pill awakening!

--Don't let alcohol or drugs into your life. They will open the door for the Devourer to devour!

--Don't live for money.

--Always find some way to encourage those around you. Most everyone feels beaten down or defeated.

--Don't be overly sarcastic. It gets old.

--Keep your living costs low regardless of your salary. Give away the rest to people in need.

--There is no excuse for having a Lamborghini or a Rolls Royce while living in a starving world. I even question my Hyundai…

--If you are going to buy furniture, buy something you will most likely keep forever.

--You don't have to have a spouse, kids or pets to have a happy life.

--In public speaking, keep it to 20 minutes and under if you want people to listen. Better to cut yourself off at this point and have people beg you to continue than to keep going on and on with "indispensable" information.

--Crushed hopes can kill anybody and anything. Dream Death is a casket made for two.

--Stop the attempt to realize your financial potential. It will drive you mad.

--Be unimpressive. It is unconstraining.

--You can always thank God for the absence of bad. You should also always thank Him for the absence of worse and worst-case scenarios. (In other words, don't take 'decent' and 'okay' for granted.)

--Complaining is not a skill to be proud of. It is missing the mark big time.

--Small decisions can be just as crucial as supposedly big ones.

--Miracles are short-lived. Everyone who gets healed ultimately dies.

--Buying a bigger house is not necessary or fun. More to clean. More to fill up. More to decorate. More to move when the time comes.

--Have a job while looking for a better job. Employers can smell the desperation of the unemployed.

--Be an amazing gift-giver.

--Ever heard of a *coup d'état*? Suggestion: Every year, enact a *coup d'you*. Forcibly overthrow any false ideas and worldview 'generalissimos' who have climbed in and claimed space in your heart and mind. Self-perceive, introspect and restore the Jesus monarchy afresh.

--Who cares if people think you are weird as long as you balance it with being kind?

--Accepting Jesus as Lord is only the beginning. It's swallowing the Red Pill. What happens after digestion?

--The Road less traveled might be that way for a good reason. Don't assume it's always the right one!

--Facing your fears is not always the best idea. Sometimes it is best to back off and walk away from things that scare you.

--When you are sick or broken, be amazed this is not your normal state and be thankful that most of your bodily systems are working properly.

--Do not let pressure overtake you. Better to step away in your prime than snap in half under your own perfectionist demands.

--Everything looks perfect from far away.

--Choose your causes wisely.

--Give your money to homeless people who ask, if for no other reason than to say, "Hey, you had the guts to ask a stranger for money and so ye shall be rewarded."

--Don't justify your lack of generosity to the homeless by saying they will only spend your donation on drugs or alcohol. Of all people who need some escape, don't you think they do?

--Pay attention to the direction you are moving rather than your immediate location.

--Feeling useless. Feeling unable. Feeling like you have nothing of value to offer. These feelings will lead to grand self-judgment and utter loneliness. This mindset is the path of daily depression and it forms the strongest reason to give up. Know that you are innately valuable — remind yourself every day!

--Some people are born with five queens on their chessboard and some with only pawns. It's not what they start with but how they play them that matters.

--Never let celebrities sway you about anything important.

--Read world news at least once every week and note how the majority of the world is suffering deeply.

--Avoid pornography. It can own you and destroy your life.

--While dining with others, pick up the restaurant tab often.

--Be patient everywhere and no matter what.

--Keep up with technology, but don't let it dominate your existence.

--Fight hard against sex trafficking (Both the Supply and the Demand.)

--Don't make decisions based on what feels good.

--Don't make decisions based solely on advice you're given by others even if the "others" are known for being wise. Always inquire of the Lord.

--Erosion plus inertia plus time equals Grand Canyons in nature and in life. How many deep cuts are happening in your world due to culture's consistent wear and tear? What is eroding you?

--Blind spots while driving cause us to wreck other cars. Our personal blind spots are far worse—they cause us to wreck others' lives. Carefully adjust your mirrors and look over your shoulder before attempting to merge.

--Be a Bible expert. By expert, I mean know the Word like the back of your hand AND do what it says.

--When you make a mistake, don't cover it up. Admit what you did. Come clean as soon as you can. Covering it will just make it blow up bigger later.

--Almost every realistic worst-case scenario for your life is actually not that bad. So, don't fear when it seems that the ground is caving in beneath you.

--If you say you are going to do something, do it.

--Don't be a critic AND ignore most critics. But know that a critic is only a stone's throw away.

--Don't put pressure on others — especially kids.

--Understand how you are typically tempted and be extremely wary of what works to bring you down. Then, never let yourself be convinced that any of these things can be good for you in any way or in any measure. No matter how well your temptations are marketed, do not even taste a sample.

--As an adult, do not attend any children's sports event and scream mean things at the kids, the referees or anyone else. If you do shout, shout encouragements only!

--Don't be defensive or easily triggered.

--Don't cancel people.

--Before you say anything about someone else, get to know them if you're able to do so.

--When dealing with anyone suffering with grief and/or loss, do not cliché them to death…and don't try to talk them out of their pain. Just because their struggle makes you uncomfortable, doesn't mean you need to try and fix it.

--Brush your tongue and the roof of your mouth with toothpaste in the morning and after coffee and in the mid-day. If you let your tongue get stinky, you will be placed on people's "someone to avoid" list because they cannot hold their nose long enough to exchange even the briefest pleasantries with you.

--Don't be super competitive. It's annoying. Play to win, but don't act like what you are trying to win matters that much.

--Hang out with God for as long as possible every day if you get the chance. There is no better place on earth than in God's presence. The best theology is found by being with the Theos and then letting Scripture tell you about Him.

--Never give a minimum wage worker a hard time.

--Don't say you will move to another country if some candidate you don't like wins President, unless you actually mean to go. I'll be happy to buy you the one-way, non-refundable ticket to Moscow, but you gotta promise you will stay, comrade. Spasibo. Enjoy Putin.

--Sometimes a dog returns to its vomit even if it has a better food option—at least this dog has.

--As soon as you feel your first cold symptoms coming on, take "Kick-Ass Immune Support," oregano oil, grapefruit seed extract, zinc and vitamin C.

--Jesus existed long before He was birthed onto the earth. He is eternal. So, watch out for people who discount the Old Testament because 'Jesus' never said this or that. Uh, yeah, He actually did. He was not the dissenting opinion when the Father and the Holy Spirit sent out the laws governing people. It was *always* unanimous.

--Bread and Circus still applies. Except now, it's AYCE buffets and big-screen streaming that numbs the mind of the populace.

--Every system is flawed...even democracy.

--Get your own word from God. What He told Peter about putting out into deep waters, He didn't tell you. What He told Moses about going to Pharoah, He didn't tell you. Don't carjack their narratives and turn them into principles for your own life.

--Don't be a roly-poly. Never be easily frightened, rolled-up or moved.

--Flashback News: 185,000 Assyrian warriors were wiped out in one night by one angel. Just a friendly reminder.

--Going to a hospital nowadays almost always guarantees bigger sicknesses and incurable infections. So why go into huge amounts of debt for that? (Yes, there are exceptions…)

--It's never too late to switch careers. Do life-giving things with your days and nights.

--Be thankful for life famines — they can bring prodigals back home.

--Before taking off on a flight, always remind yourself that this might just be it. After all, you're about to hurtle through the air, 35,000 feet above the ground, at 400 mph in a metal tube made by fallible humans. If that isn't enough, consider this man-made contraption is being piloted by another fallible human. Actually, go ahead and embrace death as a very real possibility at the beginning of every day.

--Don't take any hobby too seriously — especially golf.

--Revolutions are unimportant to most people until their power is challenged, their business is in the crosshairs, their cul-de-sac gets attacked and their head is firmly in a guillotine.

--Have 'small feet' and they will not likely be stepped on. In other words, do not be easily offended.

--See through the political rhetoric on all sides of an issue. Everyone is working an angle. Don't get spun!

--Don't be the guy who always says, "I told you so."

--Don't get nervous about speaking in public…most people in the audience aren't listening anyway. They're just praying you keep it short and likely won't recall anything you say beyond the day.

--Keep a detailed dream journal. Your subconscious mind is fascinating and weird.

--Jonah ran from God, but the consequences of his actions affected others' lives and property. Don't let your rebellion rock others' worlds.

--Maintain a stranger/alien mindset. This world isn't your forever home.

--When caught up doing the 'things you hate', you will need more than forgiveness. You will need rescue that only God can provide through Jesus.

--Some fall short of God's glory by centimeters and some by solar systems. But the Lord covers every shortfall distance at the cross.

--Refuse to be a soundbite.

--Hope deferred certainly does sicken the heart. But hope completely deleted removes the heart and defeats the man once and for all.

--Don't be a résumé promoter.

--Everybody disappoints, including you.

--One accusation — even if false — can destroy a person.

--Most prostitutes and beggars don't want to be either prostitutes or beggars.

--Humble yourself so you don't humiliate yourself.

--If someone tells you they like/love you 'just as you are,' be grateful and accept it. But pray for that person to gain better discernment and judgment.

--Avoid seed oils, sugar, grains and dairy as much as possible.

--Always be moving from Romans 7 to Romans 8.

--Do not ever worship a person or thing. It's beneath you.

--Don't ask God for what you can buy at Wal-Mart.

--Psychiatrists cannot see the chemicals in your brain, and thus, when they prescribe mind-altering drugs, you are risking your mental, emotional and physical well-being. I'd rather self-medicate and get a known effect than be medicated by someone who does not know me and end up with effects that leave me feeling worse.

--Don't talk bad about someone behind their back. Find something positive about everyone and bring that up instead.

--Depression and anxiety are cruel diseases that most people don't even have an inkling about. Ignore those who tell you to 'buck up' and 'rise above it.'

--Never say "let's do that one more time." Usually that "one more time" ends in disaster, disappointment or injury.

--There are plenty of lesser spiritual powers in this universe who will demand far less of you morally during your time on this earth. But trusting them so you can avoid discipline and popular rejection will ultimately kill you.

--Don't start another podcast. We have too many. (Mine is the official last one allowable.)

--When dealing with your teenager, always remember what a punk you were when you were their age before reprimanding them.

--Don't get cocky. Sweden used to be a superpower.

--Regularly ask people around you, 'What's the most important thing you've ever been told?'

--Anyone else have PreTSD? Our culture is such that I have trauma just thinking of our likely, future events.

--The Enneagram will not teach you much and The Secret will not help you…but feel free to waste your time and money on them and their pseudo-gurus if you like.

--I recall a time when first responders were beloved by the crowds. So, beware of being beloved by crowds. Crowds become mobs.

--Have faith in the benefits of Psalm 103.

--Don't send your meals back if there are minor mistakes and don't be a high-maintenance orderer.

--Don't ever put your drink on the same table as your laptop, unless you can guarantee it won't fall over and destroy your computer.

--Goodwill the 'somebody jacket' and wear the 'nobody hoodie' today. It looked good on Jesus and it will look good on you.

--Hell is real and apparently really rough! It's the absence of all that's good. Despite the claims to the contrary, Satan doesn't live there or rule there and it's not more fun than Heaven. So, if you thought it was going to be a party, you might want to shift your RSVP to a different sort of reservation.

--Usually the first thing people mention in conversation is what they are most insecure about or afraid of.

--Don't avoid the uncomfortable.

--Some people don't have a huge global purpose. Do the small and loving things for the people in front of you and don't wait for burning bushes.

--We are lucky that God only gave us one way to get to Heaven. He made it as simple as possible — why do we always try to complicate things to suit our own desires?

--When you make decisions that make you feel deep shame and regret, respond like Peter and not like Judas. Mourn and then move forward. There is a way forward, I promise you.

--The church is imperfect and its people are imperfect. Don't let those realities be an excuse for you to stand outside of it and judge it. Get inside and use your gifts to improve it.

--You have the Law and the Prophets and the Savior and the Spirit – You have less excuse than anyone ever has throughout history. You should know how to act and how to be so that God is pleased.

--Jesus is not a Capitalist.

--David did not defeat Goliath. God did. Just FYI. God is the hero in every story — not some man or woman. Always beware of who you call your hero.

--If you have no God-identity, you will be on a constant search for a worldly one. Trust me, that search is a cruel one if you're unable to perpetually offer this world something it finds valuable.

--These days Thoreau, Emerson and Nietzsche would simply be bloggers with small followings.

--Some addictions are culturally acceptable while others are 'offensive' and 'prove' that the addict is a piece of crap. But everyone is an addict. Everybody relies on a crutch. Let him who is without a crutch cast the first stone.

--A serum called Shilajit is the shiznit. Get to know your Himalayan superfoods (and actually, never use the word shiznit).

--If you are going to go in debt, do so to make the world a better place.

--Don't let your heart hold fast to anything that is not God. Ask Solomon about his 1000+ women.

--Obedience is saying yes to God's best life. It's actually setting yourself up for what feels best.

--Learn at least one other language.

--Deliverance is a consistent refusal to receive the enemy's deliveries. Don't answer calls or knocks from people you don't know.

--Be a lifelong learner of things that can be applied to your afterlife.

--Living without vision or purpose is too hard.

--Buy a scale and check out your weight at least weekly. It's easy to become obese and this is terrible for your internal organs. Adding on just 5 pounds per year will make you 100 pounds heavier in only 20 years.

--Every God-follower on the planet is supposed to feel a deep sense of mourning that they are not experiencing the world as it was intended to be. Real Jesus disciples are not smiling all the time. They might be daily grinding out a simple existence of obedience until the skies split open.

--Most conferences are a waste of time and money, but if it's someone else's money and you're getting paid for the time, make the most of the chance to travel and meet new people.

--Always take Phenergan with you on trips to Mexico. I advise this after not having it one time, getting Montezuma's Revenge and vomiting out around 700 gallons of food, liquid and organs in a car on the drive back to Texas. (Actually, always have Phenergan on hand wherever you are.)

--American Politics is controlled by rich, connected people who want to make the rules for the rest of us.

--The system for American elections is bad. The options for representatives are limited to people we don't know and who don't know us. I wouldn't choose for most of our leaders to be our leaders. The only candidates we get to choose from are the wealthy and/or connected people who can afford to run a campaign. You won't ever see a poor, wise man in an elected government position.

--Corporations run the gameboard and their media dice are weighted to only hit their numbers.

--Best way to fight back against corporate tyranny is to stop using their services. Bleed them dry. Without us using their goods and services, they cannot make it. But most are addicted to their 'bread and circus' and thus cannot imagine a life without the "fun" and "convenience" they offer. Either get off of social media and stop buying their ads or quit complaining when they run you.

--Is it soon becoming time to Sodom and Gomorrah us? We are most definitely arrogant, overfed and unconcerned enough to salt pillar us, right?

Less Deep but Very Practical Thoughts and Advice

--Wash your sheets and pillowcases once a week.

--Long beards and dreadlocks are hard to pull off when seeking employment. Jobs often come down to hair.

--White teeth on a straight smile put you at the top of the interview list. Vanity rules office spaces.

--Find someone who can handle your anti-résumé with grace and confidentiality.

--Don't ask people to help you move residences twice in one year if you want them to remain your friends. (Do a double move in one year with the same helpers and you will become a "caller ID" casualty.)

--Never agree to do The Master's Cleanse. I did it because my wife thought it would be fun to pour gallons of saltwater down our throats together every morning. As it turns out, it wasn't fun.

--Never count on the Academy Awards to get it right.

--When playing Risk, always aim to conquer all of Australia first and build from there.

--When in Vegas, don't play slots or Blackjack unless you want to lose your money super-fast. Learn to play Texas Hold-Em.

--Expect your Pocket Aces to be cracked.

--Don't bring a basket full of groceries to an express line.

--Star Wars is not that great. Let's just go ahead and admit that.

--Don't let other people add weight to your bar. Lift what you want. Or live weightless.

--To win on Jeopardy, memorize the map, know Shakespeare characters, watch Sportscenter, read Uncle John's Bathroom Readers and study summaries of the top 100 books ever written.

--Ball control is the key to Foosball success.

--Learn several line dances.

--Tip at least 20% no matter what.

--Always help fellow golfers search for their errant golf balls.

--Take a crazy vacation to an interesting place every year with your spouse, sibling or best friend and live it up.

--Buy comfortable underwear and creative socks.

--Do not mistreat penguins or kids.

--Go on a game show if you can.

--Wear interesting hats.

--Don't get tattoos. Find a different way to express yourself other than conformity to an ink stain.

--Never feel sorry for an athlete who doesn't get a 'market-value' contract. They are probably doing just fine unless they are a pole vaulter.

--Avoid Time-Share Presentations.

--Learn to fix a flat, change your oil, drive a stick shift and back up with a long trailer attached to your hitch.

--Listen to new music — give it a shot…same with old music.

--Learn the basics of tennis, golf, ping-pong, foosball, skee-ball and crane games.

--When bowling, use a cool bowling nickname on the scorecard. Also, on your follow-through, always finish with your bowling hand like you're combing your hair and kick out your alternate leg. It looks so cool.

--If you always dress your age, you will get old fast.

--Be willing to pay for the most amazing mattress and pillow you can possibly afford. Sleep is medicine!

--Sushi is your friend if you are at a restaurant near the coast. Sushi is your enemy if you live in Lubbock, Texas and must buy it from the grocery store.

--Avoid anyone who says: "Trust the Universe" or "Cosmic."

--The Karate Kid Crane Kick does not work too well in your average bar brawl. Leave that one in the dojo.

--Don't ever start trying to win tickets at a Chuck E. Cheese type establishment. You will spend your hard-earned money on 'winning' a $1.59 Pez dispenser and a used stuffed animal. (Apply this to Las Vegas casino games, as well.)

--When you sing Karaoke, always start with ABBA or The Bee Gees.

--If you do the tooth fairy thing with your kids, leave a set of plastic vampire teeth along with your monetary donation just to see how they process it.

--Thank God every day you have access to a private flush toilet with ample toilet paper.

--Make sure the gym treadmill is turned off before you step onto it.

--Create impossibly difficult passwords for your everything. And keep them written down with pen and paper in duplicate.

--Don't go on cruise excursions alone and don't start conversations with people at hotel ice machines.

--Occasionally and without explanation, wear a tuxedo to work.

--Michael Jordan is the GOAT. Lebron is the LLAMA. (In truth, GOATs don't matter much and debates about them are silly.)

--Little Bunny Foo Foo is a slow learner and a recidivist. Don't be like him.

--A truly talented person can kill flies on their first swing of a swatter. It's timing, power, and stealth in perfect harmony.

--I know it looks glamorous but being a Putt-Putt Professional is not as stellar as it seems at first glance.

--If you don't want the pressure of being a best man or maid of honor, start flaking hard on close friends who are in serious relationships.

--Always have ample 12-volt batteries and a non-rickety ladder so you can replace the Duracells that go out at 3 a.m. in your smoke detectors. You will not be able to sleep through the beeping.

--Amusement parks are usually made up of long lines, high prices and broken rides. Anticipate the 'fun' based on that info.

--How does one become a store Santa? There's a documentary in there somewhere.

--Never be the first client for a new chiropractor.

--Performing the Heimlich Maneuver on your boss doesn't have to change your relationship.

--Learn how to hack computers just in case.

--Do some basic study in handwriting analysis. Impress family and friends.

--You can't trust any man who allows a dog to lick his face. Watch a dog long enough and you'll see those aren't kisses.

--I've never finished a TV show that changed my life.

--Punching inanimate objects, like vending machines or brick walls, reveals your need for therapy.

--Filling up your cup with soda when you only paid for water is not criminal, but it is sad. Sneaking Dollar Store candy into a movie theater, however, is patriotic and praiseworthy.

--Mike Tyson said, "Everyone has a plan until they get punched in the mouth." My plan is to never put myself in a situation where getting punched in the mouth by a face-destroyer is probable. Standing up to bullies and heavyweight champs is way overrated.

--Never start a conversation with a 'stall neighbor.'

--In tennis, learn to be an effective pusher and lobber. You can drive your opponent insane simply by 'moonballing.'

--Horse-drawn carriage rides might seem apropos for a romantic date. But you probably won't enjoy the view or the smell of tumbling dung apples before a candlelit dinner.

--If you enjoy suffering, purchase IKEA furniture and attempt to assemble it alone. If you assemble it with your spouse, prepare for a blowout argument.

Last Words

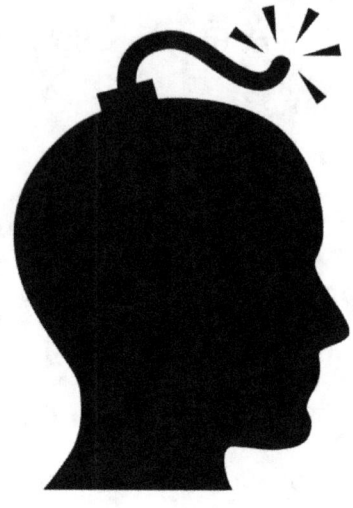

It has been a pleasure writing out all of the things I think I think for you. I hope you enjoyed it. Even more, I hope this book got you to start thinking about what you think.

It doesn't matter if you agreed with everything (or anything) you read. What matters is that you got your brain moving so it can think better about the world you exist inside of. Too few people know what they think and even fewer actually know why they think what they think.

I hope you are now one of the few who is now thinking clearly and with good reasons.

Two final recommendations I have for you as you complete this book:

1. Set up a well-thought-out Perspective or Worldview like I did with my Per'speck'tive. Build this based on your most

vital beliefs. (If you don't have significant beliefs, you might consider these first. My beliefs are Biblical. What are yours?) Then use this perspective (worldview) as a filtering system for all of your daily circumstances. This can keep you feeling more grounded and consistent even when life gets a bit crazy.

2. Go through each thought I presented and decide what you think about them. If you agree with one, determine why. If you disagree with one, determine why not. I hope that you become a Thinker with good reasons for your thoughts who can then write your own version of this book.

Well, I guess that is it from me. It was nice to meet you. See you soon.

Be Blessed and Think Well!

ABOUT THE AUTHOR:
Ben Donley

Seasoned Life Coach, Ordained Spiritual Director, Genre-bending Author, Relationship Guide and self-proclaimed Deep Thinker, Ben Donley permanently exists in Lubbock, Texas after living everywhere from Guangzhou, China to Los Angeles, California.

Ben, a Bible-believing Christian, credits God for helping him overcome addiction, severe depression, anxiety and panic disorder.

Intimacy with the Lord, love for others and compassionate justice (especially for sexually-trafficked children) are his priorities.

"The Things I Think I Think" is his 10th book.

If you liked this book, give it a five-star review and check out some of his others:

*I Guess I Do: Volume One (Pre-marriage)
*I Guess I Do: Volume Two (Post-marriage)
*The New Christian Whatever
*Unplugged: A Matrix Study

And if you are looking for a good blog or podcast or just want to communicate with Ben, check out his site at **thethingsIthinkIthink.com**.

The Things I Think I Think | Ben Donley

www.ingramcontent.com/pod-product-compliance
Lightning Source LLC
Chambersburg PA
CBHW070042230426
43661CB00005B/725